CODING UNPLUGGED
Playing with Data
ALIX WOOD
score
+1

Produced for Scholastic India by Alix Wood Books
Designed by Alix Wood
Editor: Eloise Macgregor

ISBN 978-93-5954-700-8

Published & Distributed in India by Scholastic India Pvt. Ltd.

This reprint edition: June 2025

Printed in India at MicroPrints India, New Delhi

Contents

How Can I Learn Code?

You don't need a computer to begin to learn code. This book will show you all the basic skills that you need to get started.

You'll learn to break down a problem into simple steps.

Then you can turn those steps into instructions.

Learn how to check your instructions for problems.

And then test and rewrite your code.

These are the skills you need to write code!

There are lots of different coding languages.

SCRATCH BLOCKLY LUA

RUBY JAVA ALICE PYTHON

This book helps you understand how all coding languages work.

They all work in a similar way.

You Just Need

- a pencil and paper
- a friend
- household items

Why program a computer when you can PROGRAM A FRIEND?

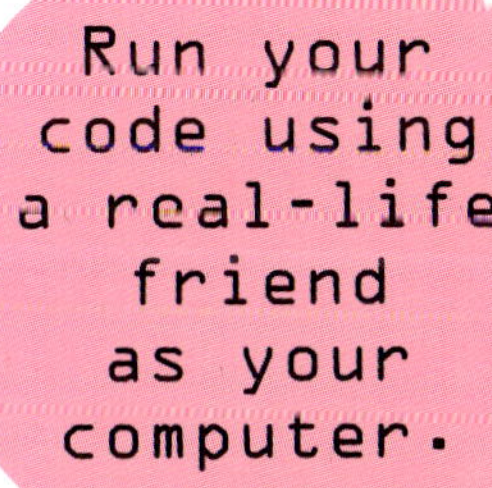

What Is Code?

Computer code is a list of instructions that tells a computer what to do.

Put on left sock

Put on right sock

The instructions must be really clear. A computer can't guess what you mean.

Try your skills by **programming** a friend.

The perfect friend does EXACTLY what the instructions say. They mustn't help by guessing what you meant.

What is Data?

2

All the information a computer is given is called data. Data could be words, pictures, numbers or sounds.

What Type?

You need to tell the computer which type of data to expect when you write code. If your code expects you to type the number '2', and you type the word 'two', your code will not work.

PROGRAM A FRIEND

3

RED

Play this data type game. Write the numbers 1 to 5 on separate pieces of card. Then write the name of four colours on separate pieces of card. Shuffle and place the cards upside down. Give your friend this instruction:

Jump up and down [   ] times

Turn a card over. Is it the right data type to run your code? Score a point if it is.

BLUE

BLUE TIMES?

Playing With Data

How do computers get the data?
We give them data in different ways.

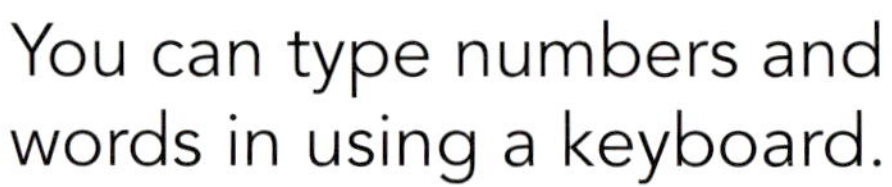

You can type numbers and words in using a keyboard.

You can upload a photo.

You may draw a picture using a mouse.

You can record sounds.

Computers turn the data into something they understand. Computers use electrical parts called transistors. Transistors are like switches. They just have two states. They can either be on or off. 0 = off, and 1 = on.

Computers use 0s and 1s to stand for all the letters, sounds, numbers and pictures that it handles!

PROGRAM A FRIEND

Can just two states do anything useful?
Yes they can! Find out how with this car spotting data game. First, create a colour chart like this.

Give your friend the chart and a pencil and go outside to watch cars. Shout out the colour of each passing car. Your friend must shade in a square in that colour's column.

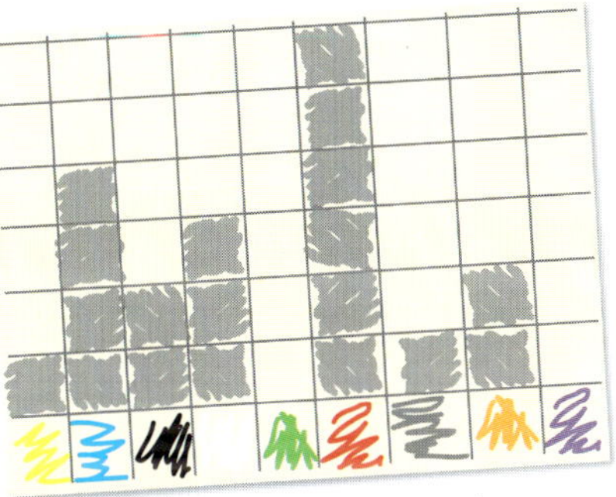

Your chart just uses two states: shaded squares, and unshaded squares.

But, this simple data tells you which colour car is popular in your neighbourhood!

Using just 0s and 1s to write code is hard. Computer scientists created computer languages to help us write code more easily.

Simple as 1, 2, 3, 4

1

8

12

0

200

There are different types of number. Numbers, such as 1, 2, 3 and 4, are called **integers**. Integers are whole numbers. They don't have decimal points, like 1.5. And, they don't have fractions, like 1 ½.

decimal point

fraction

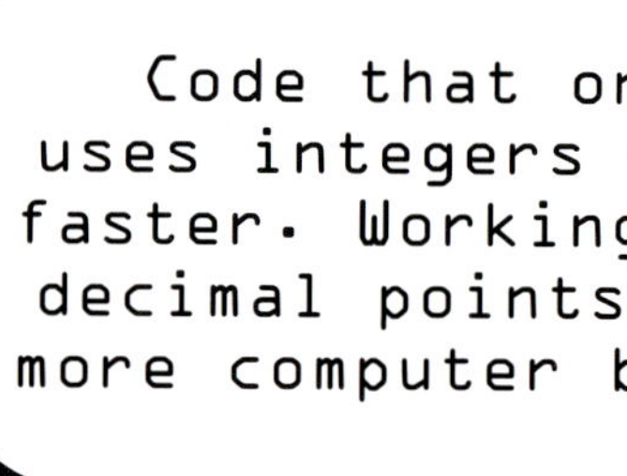

I ♡ integers

WRITE some CODE

Which of these pieces of code will work using integers?

a) I have ( ) dogs

b) The giraffe is ( ) metres tall

Answers are on page 32

PROGRAM A FRIEND

Play this 'Guess the Integer' game. Take it in turns to think of a number between 1 and 10. The other player must guess what your number is.

If the guess is greater than your number, say "greater". If the guess is less than your number say "less". How many turns does it take for your friend to guess the number?

Coders use symbols to stand for "less than" and "greater than".

The symbols look like an alligator's mouth. The alligator always faces the biggest number!

WRITE some CODE

Less than < or greater than >?

Can you choose the correct symbol?

a) 3 is ______ 7   b) 9 is ______ 4

Answers are on page 32

Different Numbers

So, integers are great if you only need to work with whole numbers. But what type of number do you need to measure your giraffe?

Your giraffe is 5.5 metres tall. Typing 5 or 6 isn't accurate enough. So, your code will need to expect an in-between number, with a decimal point.

Coders call these **floating-point numbers**. That's because the point can move, depending on the question you ask in your code!

The giraffe is 5.500 metres tall

The giraffe is 550.0 cm tall

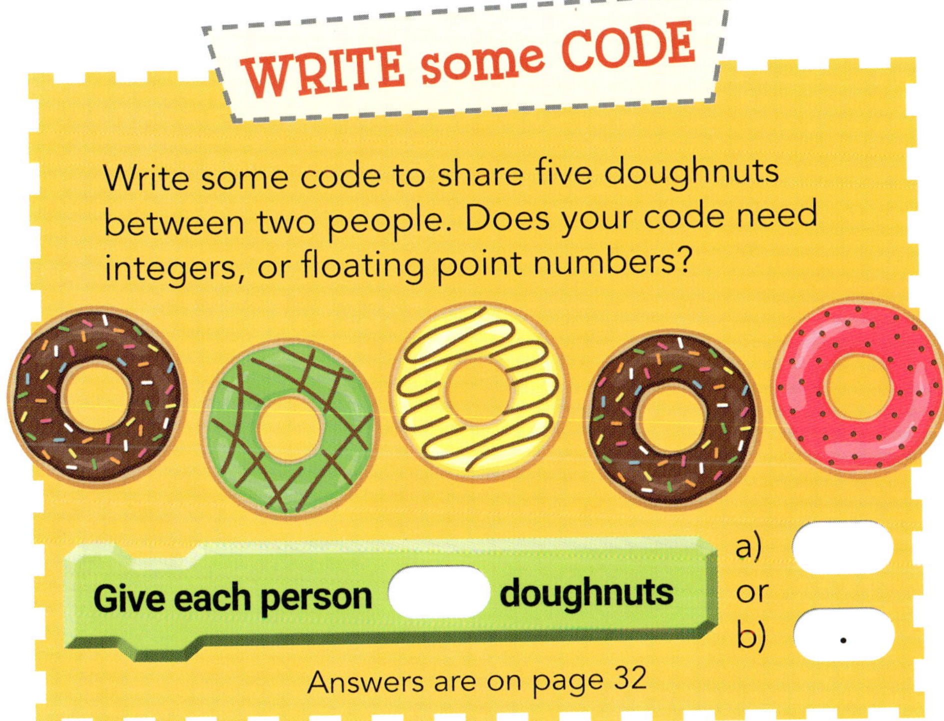

WRITE some CODE

Write some code to share five doughnuts between two people. Does your code need integers, or floating point numbers?

Answers are on page 32

Your code might need to handle **negative** numbers, too. Negative numbers are integers with a minus sign in front. If you took 7 away from 5, the answer would be -2.

Logic Data

Logic is using reason to work out if something is true or false. Computers can use their two states to answer logic questions. The answers help them work out what to do next.

PROGRAM A FRIEND

Think up some statements that are true or false. If the statement is true your friend must stand up. If the statement is false, they must sit down.

Ducks have 2 legs

The Moon is purple

If True stand up

If False sit down

WRITE some CODE

Your code needs to ask the right questions to get data to help it make a decision. Coders may plan out their logic using a diagram called a flowchart. The user, or the computer, can enter the data "true" or "false".

Try this flowchart, and find out if you are a donkey!

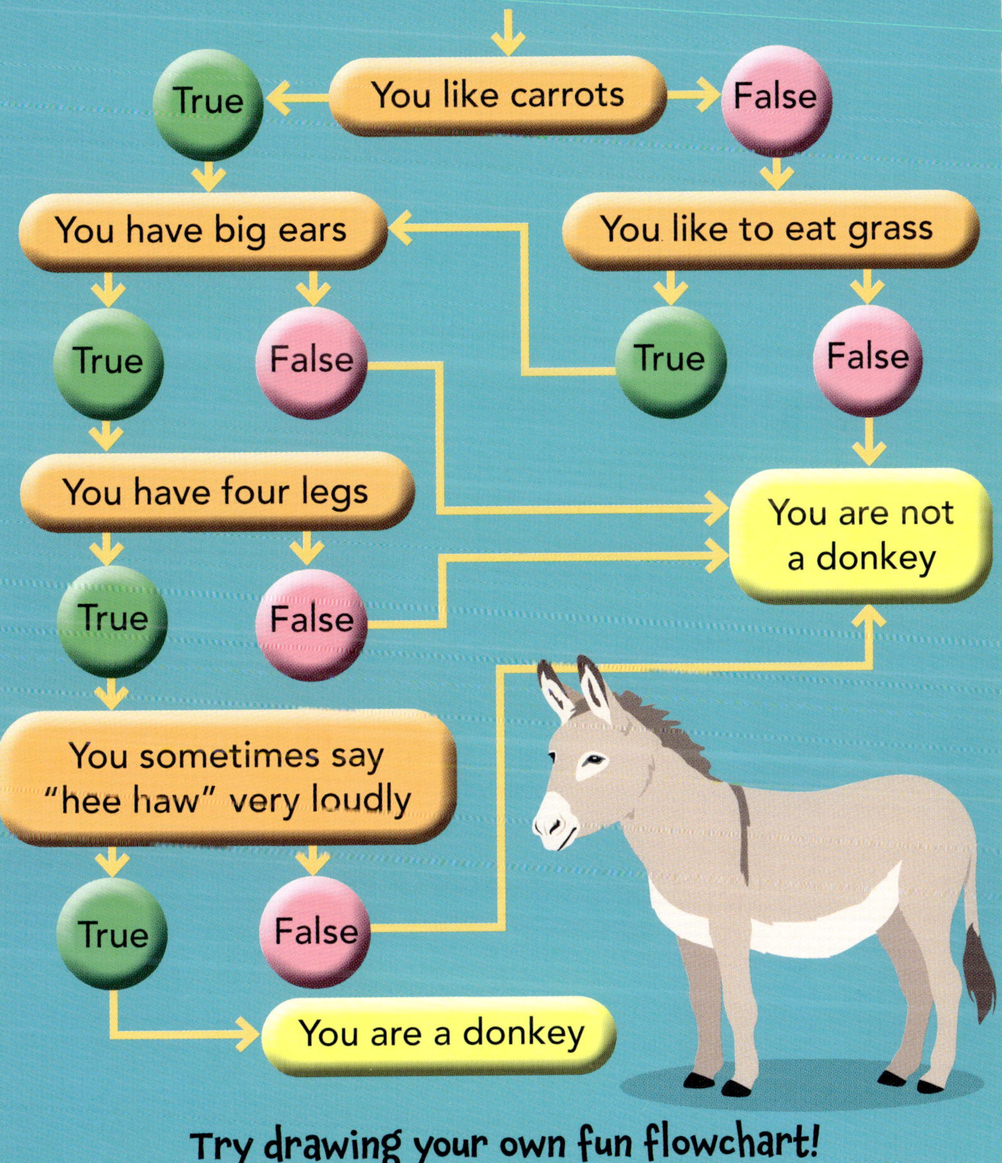

Try drawing your own fun flowchart!

Typing in the Data

A
B
C

How does a computer understand what you type? Computers use a data type known as a **character.** A character can be any letter or symbol that you type on a keyboard.

Each letter and symbol is given a number.

WRITE some CODE

This number code is called ASCII. Can you write your name using ASCII?

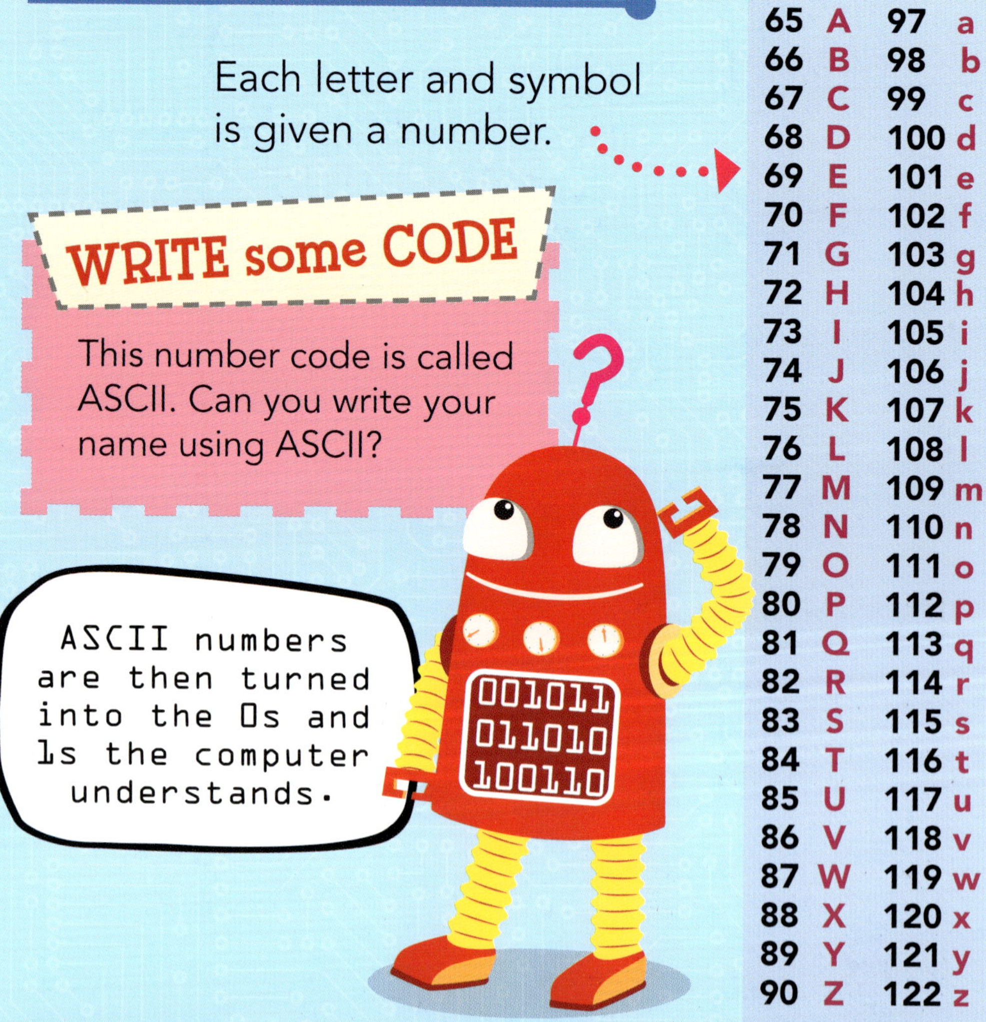

65	A	97	a
66	B	98	b
67	C	99	c
68	D	100	d
69	E	101	e
70	F	102	f
71	G	103	g
72	H	104	h
73	I	105	i
74	J	106	j
75	K	107	k
76	L	108	l
77	M	109	m
78	N	110	n
79	O	111	o
80	P	112	p
81	Q	113	q
82	R	114	r
83	S	115	s
84	T	116	t
85	U	117	u
86	V	118	v
87	W	119	w
88	X	120	x
89	Y	121	y
90	Z	122	z

You don't need to learn ASCII. Your coding language will translate the letters you type.

Characters are joined together to form a **string**. Every word you type is a string.

The computer doesn't understand words. You have to teach the computer what a new word means.

define BLINK
shut both eyes
open both eyes

PROGRAM A FRIEND

Can you write some code to tell your computer friend what these words mean?

Ask your friend to run your code. Did it work? Make your code clear, so your friend knows exactly what to do.

Answers are on page 32

How Long Is a String?

Computers sometimes need to know how long a string might be. They may need to leave enough space to display the words.

The word **party** is five characters long.

1 2 3 4 5

Some characters are invisible! Can you think of a key you press that doesn't produce a letter, number or symbol?

This string has seven characters. What character is invisible?

Answers are on page 32

Even though you can't see the character, it still counts as part of the string's length.

WRITE some CODE

How many characters do you need to display these pieces of data?

a) A box that can display **Well done!**

b) A box that can display any of the days of the week.

Monday
Tuesday
Wednesday
Thursday
Friday
Saturday
Sunday

HINT: Find the longest word to work out how many characters you need to allow.

Answers are on page 32

PROGRAM A FRIEND

Have you ever played a word tile game? Challenge your friend to a match.

What is the longest string your and your friend can make from these characters?

Answers are on page 32

Constant or Variable?

How do you tell a computer how many seconds there are in a minute? Or what your score is in a computer game? You can give **values** to pieces of data in your code.

seconds in a minute = 60

The name of the code

The value

Now, if your code asks **beep for 2 minutes** the computer knows exactly how many seconds to beep for.

BEEP! BEEP!

The number of seconds in a minute never changes. It is always 60. A piece of data that never changes is called a **constant.**

The score in a game isn't a constant. It keeps changing. To keep score in your code you use a **variable**.

A variable is a little like a box. You can store data in it.

We named our variable "score"

Our score variable adds 1 to the value each time robot scores!

WRITE some CODE

a) Can you write a piece of code to tell the computer how many minutes there are in an hour?

b) Is your code using a constant or a variable?

Answers are on page 32

Got the value wrong? You can easily fix it. Change the value and it will correct it everywhere you used the code.

Playing With Variables

Any type of data can be a value or a variable. It doesn't have to be a number. A string, such as a user name, is a variable. Different users have different names.

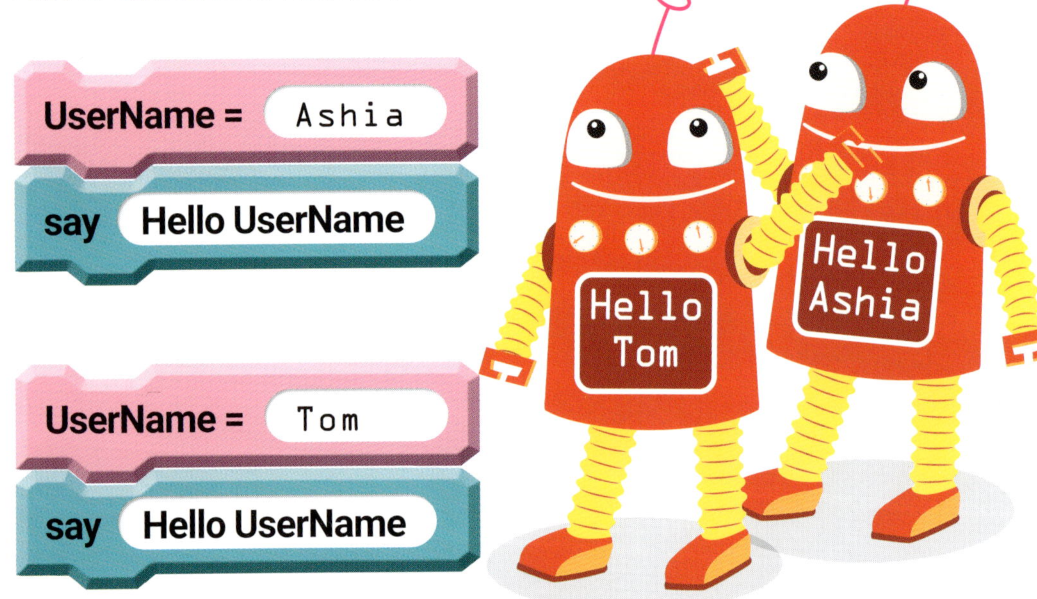

You can call up the user's name any time by typing "UserName".

WRITE some CODE

Your class teacher probably changes every year, or even every lesson. Can you create a piece of code to make a "Teacher" variable? Then, can you run it to say "Good morning" to your teacher?

PROGRAM A FRIEND

This game uses strings as variables. Your variables are 'Animal', 'Person', 'Place' and 'Action'. Label four envelopes with each variable name.

Give your friend some paper and ask them to write down some animals, people, places and actions on separate pieces of paper. Put the pieces in the right envelopes.

Animal

Person

Place

swimming

Action

Read out the story below.
Fill in the gaps with a variable from the right envelope.
Did you make a funny story?

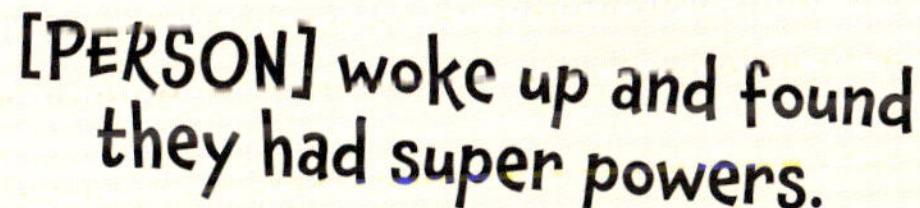

[PERSON] woke up and found they had super powers.

Now, they could fly when they were [ACTION].

They zoomed through the air and lifted a surprised [ANIMAL] off the ground.

They both flew to [PLACE] and made it their superhero base.

Bugs in Your Data!

Code doesn't always work exactly how you want, first time. Coders check and test their code to find any problems.

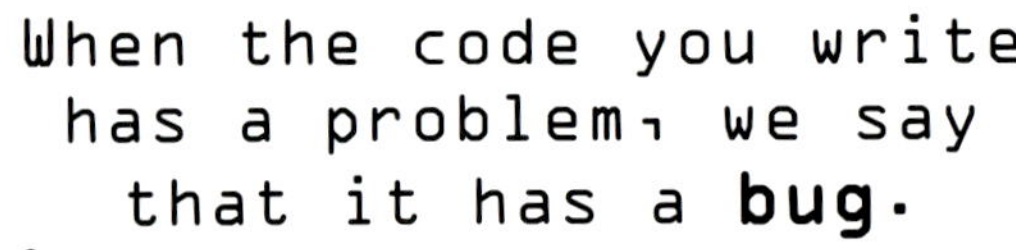

Finding and removing bugs is called debugging.

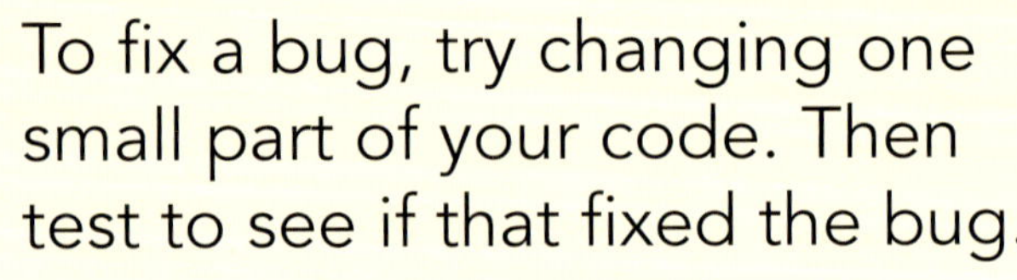

To fix a bug, try changing one small part of your code. Then test to see if that fixed the bug.

If the bug is still there, change another small part, and test it again. Keep doing this until you find the problem.

WRITE some CODE

We've taught our robot to blink.

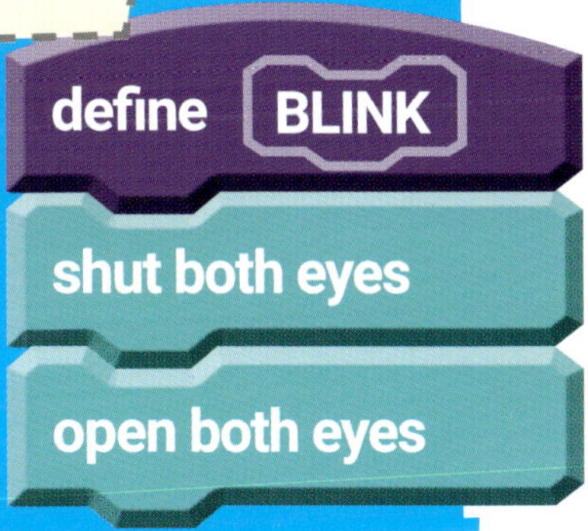

define BLINK
shut both eyes
open both eyes

This loop below asks the robot to blink five times.

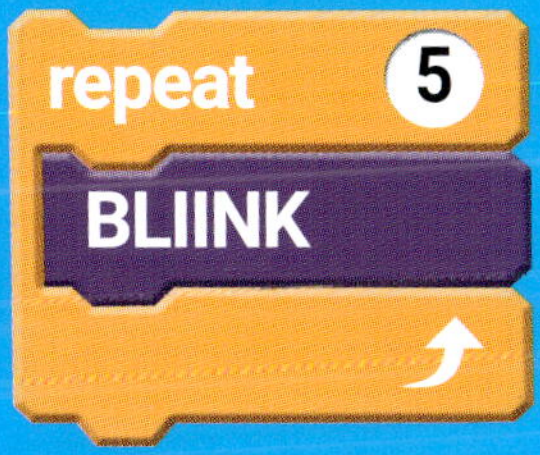

repeat 5
BLIINK

?

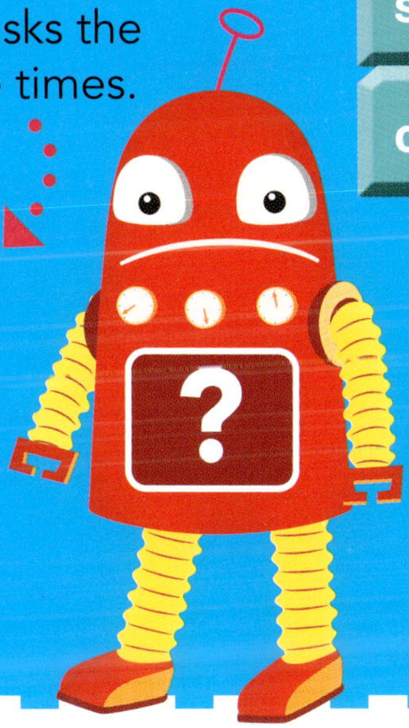

Can you see why our robot won't blink?

Answers are on page 32

Common bugs might be:

1. Spelling a word wrong.

If Troo stand up

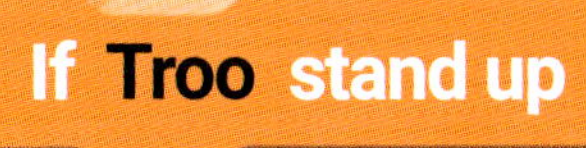

2. The logic not being right.

You are a worm?
True
Put on socks

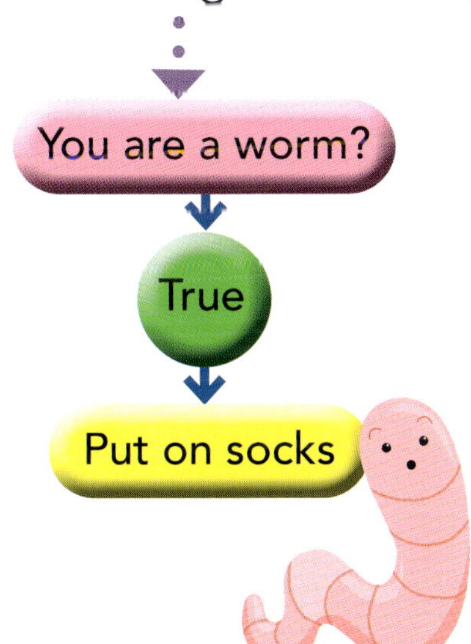

3. The code is used in a way you hadn't planned for.

Bugs happen to all coders. The best coders are always testing and fixing their code.

Making Pictures

Coders can use data to create images. The images on your screens are made up of millions of tiny blocks known as **pixels**.

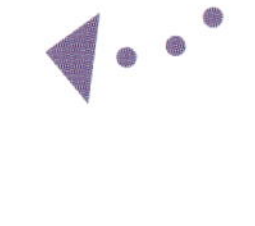

The more blocks an image uses, the smoother the picture looks.

Computer screens are measured in how many pixels, or dots per inch (dpi) they use.

On a 72-dpi screen every 1-inch (2.5 cm) square is 72 pixels high by 72 pixels wide.

WRITE some CODE

Can You Draw a Picture Using Code?

Draw a grid, with 8 rows and 9 columns, like the grid below. Each square represents a pixel. Then, use this code to draw a pixel picture. Along each row, color in any squares that have a 1. Leave the squares blank if they have a 0.

We have done the first row for you.

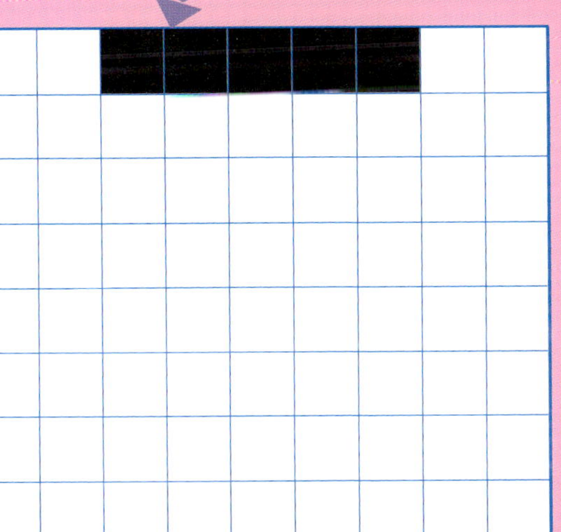

Row 1: 0, 0, 1, 1, 1, 1, 1, 0, 0

Row 2: 0, 1, 0, 0, 0, 0, 0, 1, 0

Row 3: 1, 0, 0, 1, 0, 1, 0, 0, 1

Row 4: 1, 0, 0, 0, 0, 0, 0, 0, 1

Row 5: 1, 0, 1, 0, 0, 0, 1, 0, 1

Row 6: 1, 0, 0, 1, 1, 1, 0, 0, 1

Row 7: 0, 1, 0, 0, 0, 0, 0, 1, 0

Row 8: 0, 0, 1, 1, 1, 1, 1, 0, 0

What did you draw?

Answers are on page 32

PROGRAM A FRIEND

Can you write some code to make your own grid picture? Challenge a friend to draw the image using your code. Were your instructions clear? Did the drawing work?

How Well Do You Know Data?

Take the quiz and find out.

1. Can you match the code blocks to the correct data type?

   1) string 2) sound 3) integer

   Move 10 steps
   a)

   Say Hello
   b)

   Play Drum
   c)

2. Computers turn all the data you give it into 0s and 1s so they understand it.

   a) True b) False

3. Which of these is an integer?

   a) 2.5 b) 1 ½ c) 6

4. What is a string?

   a) characters joined together to form a word

   b) a long chart

5. Which of these data types would allow you to change its value?

   a) constant b) variable

6. Can you work out what the ASCII code below says? Use the chart to help you.

89, 79, 85
67, 65, 78
67, 79, 68, 69

How did you do? Find the answers on page 32.

Glossary

bug An unexpected mistake or problem in the way something works.

character A symbol, such as an alphabet letter, used in writing or printing.

constant A number that does not change value.

seconds in a minute = 60

floating-point numbers Positive or negative whole numbers with a decimal point.

integers Whole numbers that can be positive, negative, or zero.

negative A number that is less than zero.

pixels Pixels are tiny dots or squares that makes up a digital image. Pixel is short for "picture element".

programming Writing instructions for a computer to follow.

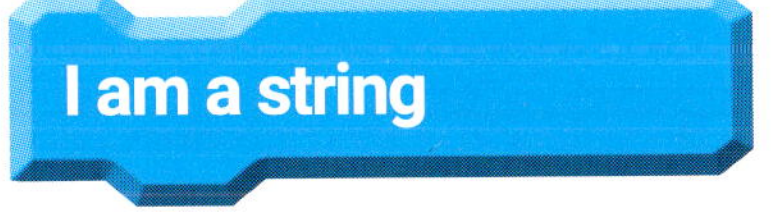

string A data type made up of characters, words, phrases, or symbols.

values The quantities of data that can be numbers, strings, or objects.

variable A named storage location in a computer program that can hold values like numbers, names or objects.

Index

Answers

p 10: a) I have 2 dogs, **p 11**: a) 3 is < 7, b) 9 is > 4, **p 13**: a) b) 2.5 doughnuts, **p 17**: WAVE - you might say "Raise one arm, move hand to left, move hand to right", WINK - you might say "Shut left eye, open left eye", **p 18**: the invisible character is the space between the words, **p 19**: top: a) you need 10 characters, b) you need 9 characters; bottom: there are two seven letter strings, toenail and elation, **p 21**: a) minutes in an hour = 60, b) a constant, **p 25**: BLIINK is spelled with two "I"s, **p 27**: You should have drawn a smiley face.

Quiz answers

1) 1b, 2c, 3a, 2) True, 3) c, 4) a, 5) b, 6) You can code